Jack in Goal

Written by Catherine MacPhail
Illustrated by Mike Phillips

Collins

Chapter 1

It was Jack's first day at Glendale School.
His family had moved because of Dad's new
job, and Jack had never felt so alone.
He wished his sister was with him, but Jess
had a tummy bug, so she was off school.

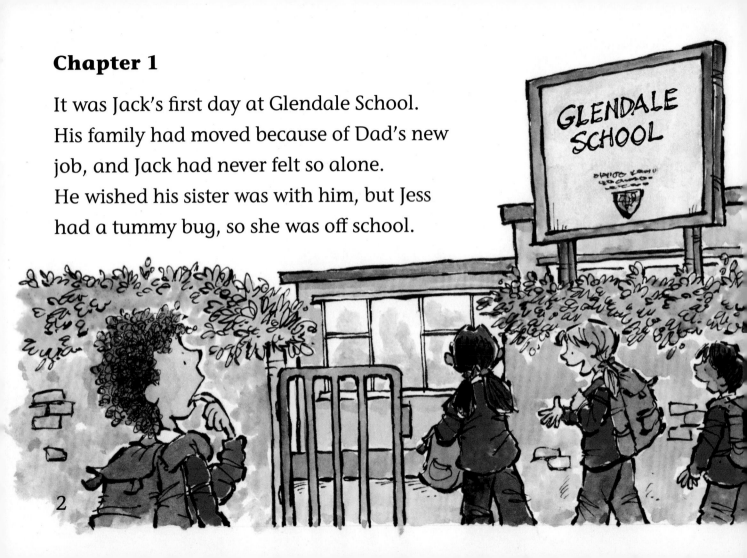

"So, you're the new kid!" said a voice, bounding over to him. "I've heard you're great at football!"

Jack looked at his teacher, Mr Sloan, in alarm. "Football?"

The teacher seemed so excited, all Jack could do was nod.

Mr Sloan grinned. "I'm the school football coach, and we're looking for a new goalkeeper in our team – it'll be great to have you on board!"

3

Everyone in Jack's new school was welcoming, but he was too busy worrying. He couldn't play football at all, but didn't want to admit to Mr Sloan that he'd lied.

"We're excited to see your goalkeeping skills!" Rob said. He was one of the children on the team. "You're coming to football training tomorrow?"

Football training? How was he going to get out of this one?

FOOTBALL TRAINING

Chapter 2

"You look like you need cheering up," Dad said, when Jack got home from school. "How about going out on the bikes?"

Jack loved going out on his bike. But he still had to come up with a plan to miss football training.

If only he could pretend to catch the bug Jess had, but Dad would never fall for it.

On Tuesday, he limped into Mr Sloan's room.
"Can't play today, Sir. I fell down the stairs."

"Oh well, you'll be fine tomorrow."

On Thursday, he walked in with a patch on his eye.
"Can't play today, Sir. Fell out of bed."

"You're very unlucky, Jack."

"I seem to be, Sir."

9

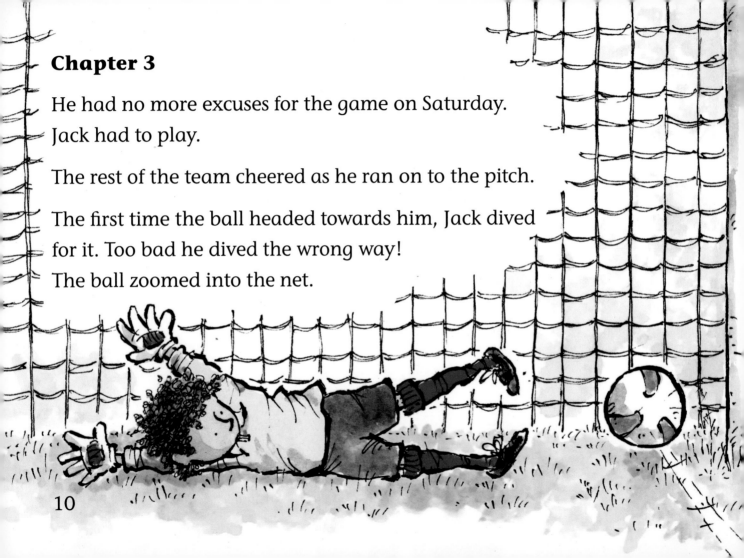

Chapter 3

He had no more excuses for the game on Saturday.
Jack had to play.

The rest of the team cheered as he ran on to the pitch.

The first time the ball headed towards him, Jack dived
for it. Too bad he dived the wrong way!
The ball zoomed into the net.

Then he dived the other way.
The ball went in the net again.

The next time he leapt in
the air to catch the ball.
It slipped through his fingers.

11

At last he grabbed the ball! But he kicked it the wrong way and scored an own goal.

In the end, he let six goals into the net.

The rest of the team didn't cheer him as they left the pitch.

"I thought you said you were good?" Rob said.

"You've just had a bad day, Jack," Mr Sloan said.
"You'll do better in the Big Match."

"The Big Match?"

"Yes," Mr Sloan told him. "We're playing our rivals,
Picton School, next week."

13

Chapter 4

At last, on the day before the Big Match, Jess felt better.

Jack had never been so happy.

The whole school was there to watch the game.

"You're going to be fine, Jack,"
Mr Sloan told him.

Jack agreed.
"I'm going to be great, Sir!"

"We haven't a chance!"
Rob moaned. "Not with him
in goal."

But this was a different Jack.

He leapt in the air and
caught the ball. He dived
this way and that. He saved
shot after shot.

With one minute to go, the score was 4–3 to Glendale.

At the very last moment, Picton got a penalty.

It was all down to Jack.

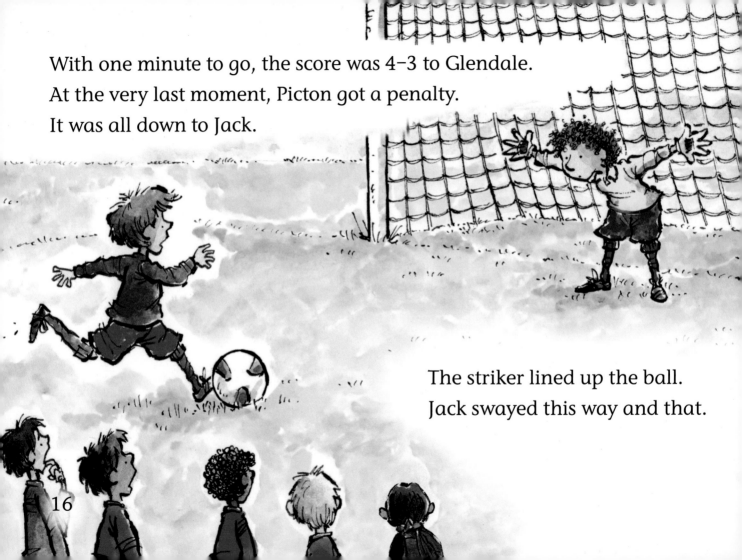

The striker lined up the ball.

Jack swayed this way and that.

The ball flew towards the top corner.
Jack leapt for it. The crowd
held their breath ...

He caught it!

The final whistle blew.

"We won!" yelled Rob.

Rob turned to Jack.
"Thank goodness you weren't completely useless this time!"

"What did you say?"

"I said, I'm glad you weren't ..."
Rob didn't finish.

Jack jumped on him.
"Take that back!"

A figure ran from the crowd. "Leave my sister alone!"

Everyone looked, and blinked. It was Jack!

But Jack was rolling on the ground with Rob.

Mr Sloan looked from Jack, to the other Jack. "What's all this?"

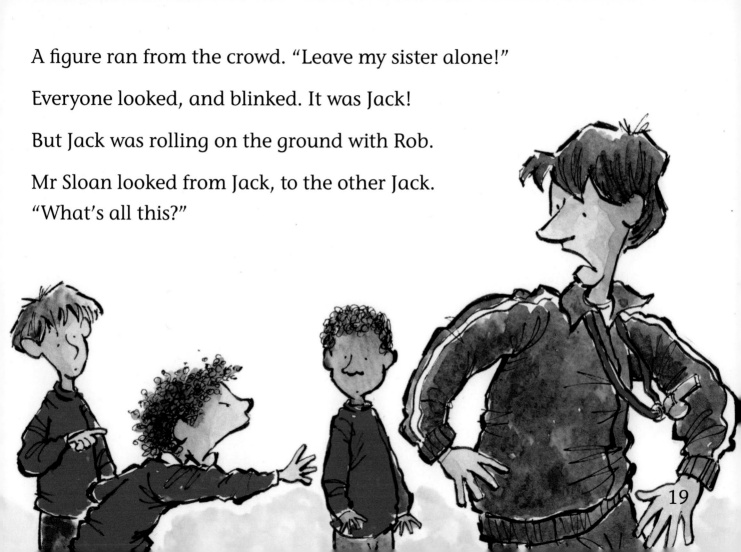

"This is my twin sister, Jess," Jack said. "She's the one who's a good goalkeeper. Not me."

Jess stood up. "We look so alike no one can tell the difference."

"I'm terrible at football," Jack continued, "I panicked when you thought I was good – I wanted to be liked on my first day. I was going to admit the truth, but didn't want to let you down for the Big Match. I asked Jess to play in goal today in my place."

Jack was sure he was in big trouble.

Jess was sure she would never play football again.

Then, Mr Sloan grinned. "Well, I think we've found our new team goalie! That right, team?"

All the children cheered. Even Rob. They carried Jess shoulder-high around the pitch.

Jack was happy; he preferred riding his bike anyway.

21

Winning moves!

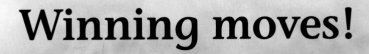

"Can't play today."

"Fell out of bed."

"I'm going to be great!"

"All the children cheered."

23

Ideas for reading

Written by Clare Dowdall, PhD
Lecturer and Primary Literacy Consultant

Reading objectives:
- continue to apply phonic knowledge and skills as the route to decode words until automatic decoding has become embedded and reading is fluent
- draw on what they already know or on background information and vocabulary provided by the teacher
- make inferences on the basis of what is being said and done

Spoken language objectives:
- use relevant strategies to build their vocabulary
- give well-structured descriptions, explanations and narratives for different purposes, including for expressing feelings

Curriculum links: Physical education, PSHE

Interest words: limped, headed, zoomed, dived, grabbed, swayed

Word count: 762

Resources: pens and paper

Build a context for reading

This book can be read over two or more reading sessions.

- Look at the front cover and read the title. Discuss what children think has happened to Jack in goal.
- Ask children to share experiences of being a goalkeeper and discuss their feelings.
- Read the blurb together. Encourage children to speculate about why Jack isn't happy and support them to make inferences based on their own experiences.